Errors of Regression Models

One Stat to Rule Them All

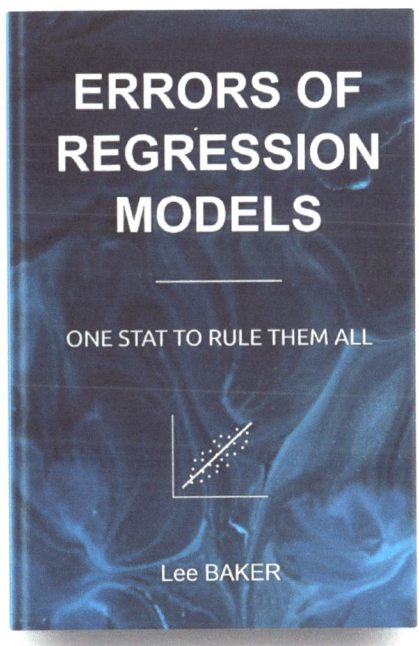

Copyright

Errors of Regression Models (1ˢᵗ Edition)

By Lee Baker

Copyright 2020 Lee Baker

Thank you for purchasing this book. You are welcome to share it with your friends.

No part of this publication may be reproduced, copied, stored in a retrieval system or transmitted in any form or by any means without the prior written permission of the publisher

If you enjoyed this book, please return to your favourite book retailer to discover other works by this author.

Thank you for your support.

***

Contents

Introduction

The Misunderstood: Errors, Residuals, Deviations

The Black Sheep of The Family: The R2 Value

The Tearaway: Variance of Residuals

The Good Twin: Mean Absolute Error

The Evil Twin: Mean Error

The Daddy: Root Mean Square Error

Jeez, That's One Dysfunctional Family!

Summary – One Stat to Rule Them All

About the Author

Video Course

Leave a Review

http://www.bit.ly/EPMCourse

Introduction

***

There's something coming through…

A picture is forming…

It's...

It's...

Gah!!! It's gone!

Sometimes, learning about statistics can be a bit like peering into a crystal ball. You think you've got it, only to read one more article/paper/blog, and suddenly it's as clear as mud again, and you're further away from the answer than when you first started.

MaxBG1001 on his blog says it's one thing, but Sk8rBoi on TwitFace insists it's something else – and they both have perfectly plausible explanations as to why they're both right. RazrButt and VanillaCupCake are saying something different again, and they sound like they know what they're talking about too!

Aaaggghhh – I'm so confused!

Choosing the correct statistic to use in any given situation can seem like a daunting task at times. When there are numerous possible statistical calculations you can do with your data, is there one answer that is correct, while all others are incorrect?

Not usually.

When you realise that there are about a dozen different ways to calculate the average value – *and they're all wrong* – it tends to give you a bit of perspective about statistics.

So here are two things that will help you find your Zen:

1. Statistics is more like a cleaver than a laser scalpel
2. There is not usually a single correct answer (or even *any* correct answer!)

In most cases there is a spectrum of approaches, some of which are more appropriate than others.

Your job isn't to make the best choices with your data – you can leave that to the experts that have a PhD in stats and 30+ years of experience. No, your job is to make sure you know how to make good choices about your data.

In this book we're going to be talking about how to choose the most appropriate statistics to measure the accuracy of your regression-based prediction model.

You'll discover that there is a family of related statistics, each member of which has their own set of dedicated fans.

Nevertheless, in this case there is one correct statistic to use, while all the other measures – while useful in their own way – give only partial answers as to how to select the most accurate predictive model.

Each of these family members will be introduced, and I'll take you through their advantages and disadvantages, and show you how to calculate and interpret all of them. Finally, I will explain *exactly* why one particular family member is The Daddy!

***

The Misunderstood:

Errors, Residuals, Deviations

Whenever I talk to statisticians, I get confused – after all, I'm just a humble scientist that sort of tripped and fell into Data Science almost by accident – and statisticians talk a completely different language. What you do notice, though, if you listen carefully, is that they are *extremely precise* about what it is they're saying. You might not *understand* what they're saying, but to other statisticians there is no ambiguity.

On the other hand, when talking about statistics with non-statisticians there always seems to be disagreements, confusion and misunderstandings, usually surrounding the terminology used.

In the world of prediction, there are always disagreements about whether the term **Error**, **Residual** or **Deviation** should be used to describe the difference between **Observation** and **Prediction**, so I wanted to clear this issue up right from the start.

Let's make a few definitions first, and then discuss what they mean.

Observations
An observation is a past or present value of something of interest you're measuring or counting during a study or experiment: **a measured value** at a certain point in time, such as a person's height or weight, or **a count of** the number of animals, people, coins or cars.

Predictions
A prediction is a statement about a future event. **Predictive modelling** is the process of applying a **statistical model** or **Machine Learning algorithm** to data

for the purpose of predicting new or future observations, also known as predictions.

OK, so that should clear up any confusion about observations and predictions – an observation is a measure or count of a variable of interest in a study, while a prediction is the outcome of a process to infer new or future observations by some mathematical means.

So, on we go to Errors, Residuals and Deviations.

Errors
The Error is the difference between an **observed value** and the **unobservable true value** of a quantity of interest, for example a population mean.

Residuals
A residual is the difference between an **observed value** and the **estimated or predicted value** of a quantity of interest, for example a sample mean.

Deviations
Deviation is a measure of the difference between an **observed value** and **some other value**. A deviation that is a difference between an observed value and the *true value* of a quantity of interest (such as a population mean) is an **error** and a deviation that is the difference between the observed value and an *estimate* of the true value (such as a sample mean) is a **residual**.

OK, so that should clear things up a bit – the error is the deviation from the 'true' value, which may not be knowable, while the residual is the deviation from a prediction of the true value.

This graphic might help a little:

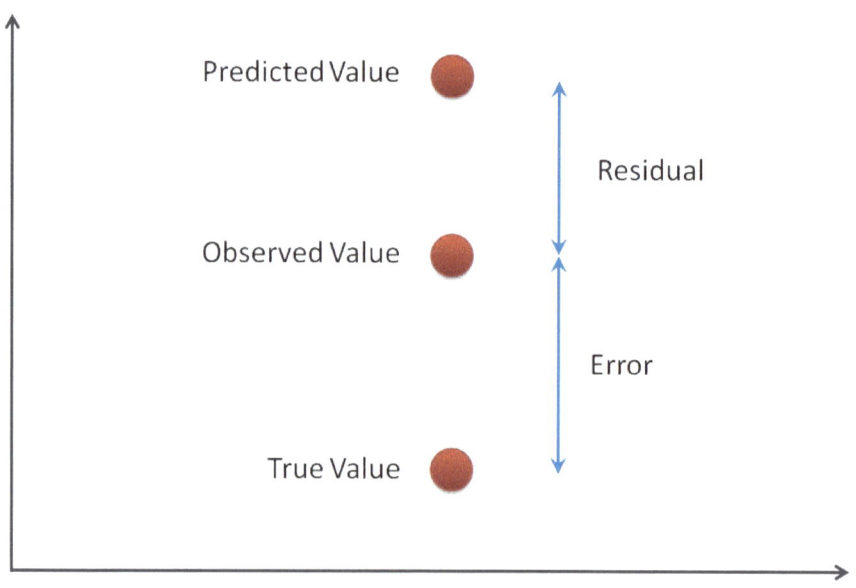

Distinction Between Residual and Error

It might seem unimportant to make these distinctions, but if you look around the literature, stats books and published papers you will often see various statistics quoted, such as **RMSE**, **RMSR** and **RMSD** (we'll come to these later), which are abbreviations of:

- Root Mean Squared Error
- Root Mean Squared Residual
- Root Mean Squared Deviation

To clarify – **these are all the same thing**, and since the error is often unknowable and the deviation is ambiguous, the correct term should be RMSR.

Despite this, RMSR is rarely used and most often you will see RMSE being used in the literature. I even got this wrong in my PhD thesis (but I got away with it!).

So what terms shall we use here? I'll try to be consistent, but I may lapse from time-to-time. Here, the terms error, deviation and residual may be used interchangeably, but don't let that fool you – **residuals** are what we're talking about!

So what are residuals in terms of a regression model? Well, a regression model will make predictions about a quantity of interest, and typically these predictions will vary – in other words, they will not likely all coincide with the observed values:

ID	Observed	Predicted	Residuals
1	0.414	0.430	0.016
2	0.412	0.420	0.008
3	0.422	0.400	-0.022
4	0.355	0.350	-0.005
5	0.313	0.330	0.017
6	0.503	0.500	-0.003
7	0.477	0.470	-0.007
8	0.532	0.530	-0.002
9	0.341	0.340	-0.001
10	0.370	0.380	0.010

Prediction Rarely Matches Observation

We can plot the predictions against the observations on a **Scatter plot**, and run a regression analysis on the data:

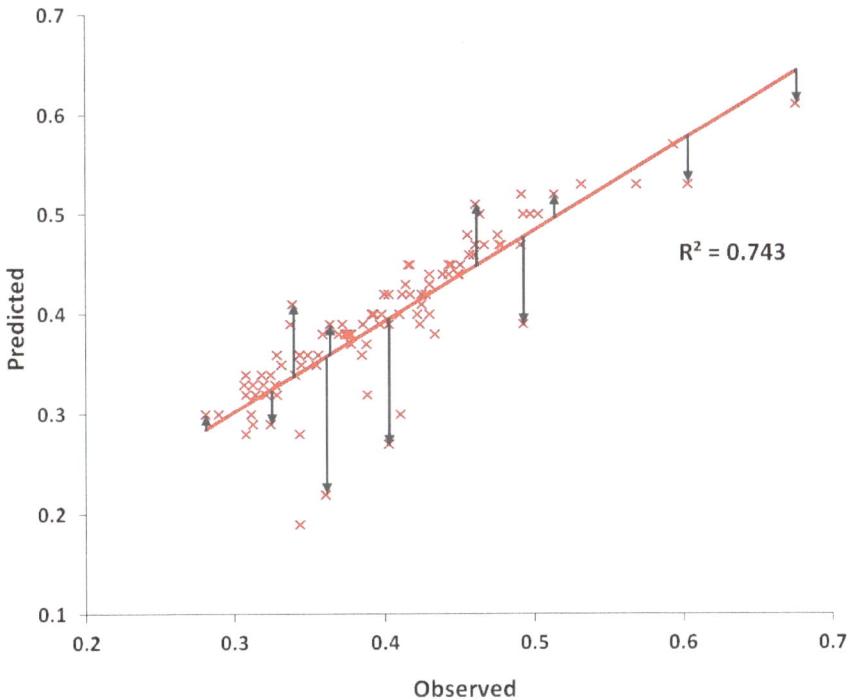

Residuals on a Scatter Plot

The residuals, marked as arrows on the Scatter Plot, are a measure of **by how much the predictions deviate from the best-fit line**.

Hopefully now we're all on the same page about what observation, prediction, error, deviation and residual all mean, we can move on to actually *do* some stuff with them.

Incidentally, there is something wrong with the Scatter Plot on the previous page. Have another look at it and see if you can spot what it is – I'll explain more in the next chapter.

***

The Black Sheep of The Family:

The R^2 Value

Did you spot the problem with the Scatter Plot?

Most people won't.

The answer is that the R^2 value is a measure that can be very misleading. Not always, but sometimes, and you need to be very sure about your analyses before using R^2 as a measure of the ability of a model to make accurate predictions.

Let me explain by way of example.

There are two different questions we might ask of these predictions:

- How far do the predictions deviate from observation?
- How far do the predictions deviate from the line of best fit?

These are actually two very different questions.

Here is a Scatter Plot of the same data as before (in red), but I've also added a replica of these data (in blue). In this second set I've reduced the size of the residuals by half (i.e. decreased the variance) and added a positive bias of 0.3:

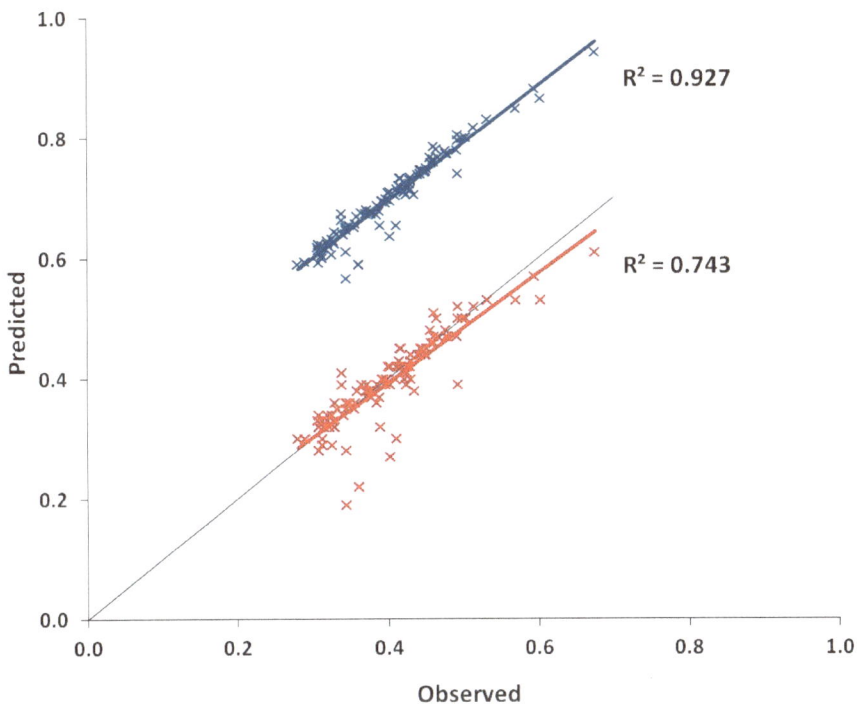

Competing Models With Added Bias and Variance

The red data group nicely around the **Line of Perfect Correspondence**, where **prediction equals observation**. In this case the line of best fit coincides with the line of perfect correspondence, and R^2 is a perfectly acceptable measure of model accuracy.

However, the data in blue are not even close to the Line of Perfect Correspondence, indicating that these predictions are very far from the observed values – and yet **the R^2 value of the blue data is very much larger than that of the red data**.

In other words, if your model produces biased predictions, then R^2 can be extremely misleading and potentially disastrously wrong!

So why can R^2 get it so wrong?

What we are interested in is measuring the deviation of the predictions **from observation**, but what R^2 measures is the deviation of predictions **from the line of best fit**.

These may be the same, but they may not. In any case, there are better ways of measuring the effectiveness of predictive models, and this is where we're going next.

***

The Tearaway:

Variance of Residuals

When it comes to measuring how much a set of numbers vary, usually one of the first things that comes to mind is the variance, as it measures **how far these numbers are spread out from their average value**, so let's have a look at the variance and see if it can help us measure the accuracy of a regression-based predictive model.

We calculate the variance of the residuals like this:

$$Variance\ of\ Residuals = \frac{\sum (Residual - Mean)^2}{N}$$

You already know how to calculate the residuals and the mean of the residuals. Well, at least I *hope* you know how to calculate the mean of the residuals – if you can't you're not really ready to be working with predictive modelling!

So after you've got these, you take the difference between them and square each result. This is an expression of how far each residual deviates from their average value. Then calculate the mean of all the results by summing (that's what the Σ means) and dividing by N, the number of predictions.

I've calculated the residuals and their variances for each of the blue and red models from the previous chapter to see whether the variance is useful:

ID	Residuals (Red Model)	Residuals (Blue Model)
1	0.016	0.308
2	0.008	0.304
3	-0.022	0.289
4	-0.005	0.298
5	0.017	0.309
6	-0.003	0.299
7	-0.007	0.297
8	-0.002	0.299
9	-0.001	0.300
10	0.010	0.305

Variance	Variance
0.00014	3.5 E-5

Variance of Residuals Can Be Misleading

If you recall, the blue model is a clone of the red model, but with reduced variance and added bias. The residuals of the red model are very much smaller than those of the blue model, indicating that the red model is much more accurate, and yet the variance of the blue model is much smaller. Intuitively, we know that the red model would be a better predictor than the blue model if it didn't have the added bias, and this is what the residual variance tells us.

On the face of it, it seems that the **residual variance is not a good measure of model accuracy** because it is a measure of the deviation from the residual mean, which is flawed when the model is biased.

That's not necessarily a reason to throw out the residual variance altogether, though – it can clearly be very useful for unbiased models.

It also has value in the fact that the units are related to those of your variable of interest (hint: think 'square-root'!). We'll come back to this in a later chapter.

For now, let's move on and take a look at something called the Mean Absolute Error.

***

The Good Twin:

Mean Absolute Error

All predictions are wrong, but it is useful to be able to measure *by how much*, and there are many ways in which we can quantify the size of the error (oops, sorry, I meant *residual*).

The **Mean Absolute Error** (which should be called the Mean Absolute Residual, but isn't) is just such a measure, and we can calculate it as:

$$ME_{abs} = \frac{\sum |predicted - observed|}{N}$$

Gah!!! That looks horrible!

OK, let's break it down and work outwards from the centre.

We already know that the difference between prediction and observation is the residual, so we can start from there.

The vertical brackets tell us that we need to calculate the **modulus of the residual**, that is, the magnitude or size of the residual, disregarding the sign. For example, residuals that have the values +3 and -3 have the same **absolute residual** of +3.

From here we calculate the mean of these absolute residuals by summing, then dividing by N, the number of predictions.

Let's have a look at the residuals of the red model to see what I mean:

ID	Residuals	|Residuals|
1	0.016	0.016
2	0.008	0.008
3	-0.022	0.022
4	-0.005	0.005
5	0.017	0.017
6	-0.003	0.003
7	-0.007	0.007
8	-0.002	0.002
9	-0.001	0.001
10	0.010	0.010

ME_{abs}
0.009

The Absolute Value of the Residual is Always Positive

The Mean Absolute Error is a measure of the **average size of the residuals** in a set of predictions, without considering their direction.

The illustration below may help to understand this concept:

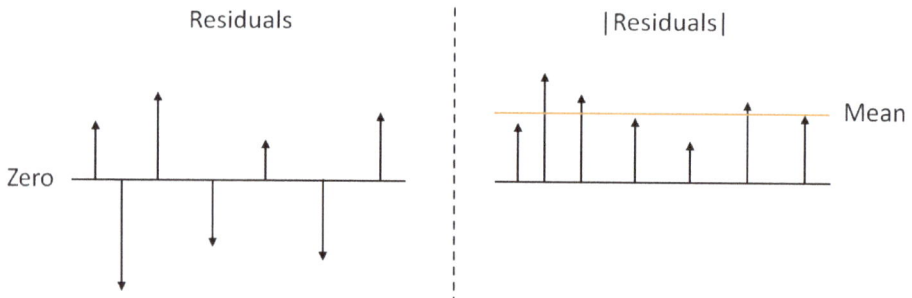

Residuals (left) and Their Absolute Values (right)

On the left are the residuals. Residuals that are positive sit above the line, whereas those that are negative sit below the line. For the absolute residuals, all the negative values are converted to positive whilst retaining the size, so the illustration on the right shows all the absolute residuals, which are all positive.

The Mean Absolute Error doesn't tell you whether or not a model is biased overall because it conveys no information about the direction of the residuals, but it does tell you by how much each prediction varies from observation, and is therefore good at expressing the **average model prediction error**, marked as the orange line on the illustration above.

Note that the units of ME_{abs} are the same as the variable of interest, so if your variable ranges from, say, 0 to 100, then the Mean Absolute Error can take possible values from 0 to 100, or even higher if you have a really bad model!

The ME_{abs} has an evil twin though, who is out to confuse you!

We will meet him in the next chapter.

***

The Evil Twin:

Mean Error

So we've had a look at the good twin, the **Mean Absolute Error**, so now let's get acquainted with the evil twin – **Mean Error**.

The Mean Error is calculated as:

$$ME = \frac{\sum(predicted - observed)}{N}$$

The Mean Error is pretty simple to work out – all you do is calculate the **mean of the residuals**, and voila! Instant evilness!

Actually, the equation looks rather innocuous, not evil at all – it's almost identical to the good twin. The only difference here is that we don't calculate the absolute residuals, we leave them just as they are.

To see how the Mean Error differs from the Mean Absolute Error, take a look at this:

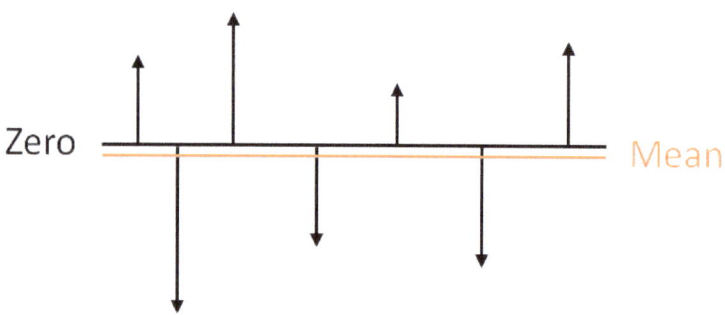

The Mean Error Can Be Negative

In contrast with the Mean Absolute Error, the residuals can be negative, and as a consequence the Mean Error can also be negative!

If we're interested in expressing the accuracy of a predictive model as some sort of *size* – as in *'it's this big'* – then the Mean Error is no good to us at all.

This is why it's the evil twin – it looks almost identical to the good twin, but it can be very confusing as to which one to believe. Worse still, Mean Error is *always* a smaller value than the Mean Absolute Error because positive and negative residuals cancel out. The Mean Error tries to seduce you (*pick me, pick me*) because we all love small error values, don't we (*oh come on, you know you want to…*)?

Actually, I'm being a little unfair to Mean Error. He's not so evil. Yes, he's confusing and seductively insidious, but he does have some redeeming qualities.

While Mean Error is not suitable for telling us the size of the accuracy, he actually does a very good job at measuring the **average model bias**.

This can be very useful. For instance, if you discover that a model has an average model bias of 75, to get a more accurate model all you need to do is subtract 75 from each prediction. It might seem unsophisticated in the world of Machine Learning and intelligent algorithms, but it's effective nonetheless!

In the next chapter we're going to meet The Daddy of the group, the Root Mean Squared Error.

***

The Daddy:

Root Mean Square Error

The prize for The Daddy of all regression-based measures of accuracy, though, has to go to the Root Mean Square Error – aka RMSE, RMSD or RMSR, depending on where you find it.

The RMSE is calculated as:

$$RMSE = \sqrt{\frac{\sum(predicted - observed)^2}{N}}$$

The RMSE is a little more complicated to work out than the other members of the family, but not too difficult for us – we're *experienced* now! All you have to do is work out the square of each residual before taking the mean and finally the square root.

When compared to the MAE, the RMSE – since the residuals are squared before they are averaged – gives a **relatively high weight to large residuals and outliers**. In other words, when large residuals are undesirable in a model, the RMSE should always be preferred to the MAE as a measure of model accuracy. On the other hand, the use of squared distances renders the interpretation of RMSE difficult, while the MAE is conceptually simpler because each error contributes to MAE in proportion to the absolute value of the error, which is not true for RMSE.

For example, if we have a pair of errors – 5 and 10 – the MAE gives us an average error of 7.5 (the mean of 5 and 10), whereas the RMSE gives us an average error of 7.9 (the square root of the mean of 5^2 and 10^2). Intuitively, we can easily understand that the average of 5 and 10 is 7.5, because it is half-way between the two points, but it is much harder to explain to your granny that the average of 5 and 10 is 7.9.

When it comes to the accuracy of regression-based models, the argument always boils down to whether you should use MAE or RMSE, so let's have a look at an example to see how they compare.

I've arranged for three competing models to all have the same total residual, and therefore the same MAE (overleaf).

As you can see, for a fixed level of bias, when the variance increases so does the RMSE. This tells us that **RMSE is a function of the model variance**. Just as importantly, MAE is neither a function of the variance nor the RMSE.

ID	Residuals (Model 1)	Residuals (Model 2)	Residuals (Model 3)
1	2	1	0
2	2	1	0
3	2	1	0
4	2	1	0
5	2	1	0
6	2	3	0
7	2	3	0
8	2	3	0
9	2	3	0
10	2	3	20

MAE 2.0	MAE 2.0	MAE 2.0
Variance 0.0	Variance 1.1	Variance 40.0
RMSE 2.0	RMSE 2.2	RMSE 6.3

RMSE is a Function of Variance

Let's have a look at another example, but this time arrange for fixed variance as we increase the MAE:

ID	Residuals (Model 1)	Residuals (Model 2)	Residuals (Model 3)
1	2	3	4
2	2	3	4
3	2	3	4
4	2	3	4
5	2	3	4
6	4	5	6
7	4	5	6
8	4	5	6
9	4	5	6
10	4	5	6

MAE 3.0	MAE 4.0	MAE 5.0
Variance 1.1	Variance 1.1	Variance 1.1
RMSE 3.2	RMSE 4.1	RMSE 5.1

RMSE is a Function of Bias

This time, for a fixed variance the RMSE increases as we increase the MAE. This tells us that **RMSE is a function of MAE**.

Putting all these observations together:

- RMSE is a function of the model variance
- RMSE is a function of MAE
- MAE is not a function of the model variance
- MAE is not a function of the RMSE

The conclusion?

Since the RMSE *contains* MAE in its calculation, it is evident that the MAE is *less capable* of fully representing the model in terms of its inherent accuracy of prediction compared with the RMSE.

That's not entirely the end of the story, though – as we shall see in the next chapter, where we pull together all members of the family for a little household get-together…

***

Jeez, That's One Dysfunctional Family!

Despite all the shouting and the arguments, there is one very good reason why RMSE is The Daddy – and I've already given you a clue what it is!

Let me introduce you to The Daddy's superhero name:

The Bias/Variance Trade-Off !!!

If you haven't heard of this, you're in for a treat, because this is *soooooo* important to predictive modelling, and gives you the **total error for any predictive model**.

The BVTO, as some might call it, is expressed as the Mean Squared Error. Recognise it? You should – it's the RMSE without the R. Or, put another way, it's $RMSE^2$.

So here it is – the BVTO is calculated as:

$$MSE = Variance + Bias^2 + Noise$$

We already know how to calculate the MSE and the RMSE, but the really important thing is that the **Bias/Variance Trade-Off is expressed in terms of both the variance and the bias (MAE)**.

This means that the accuracy of any model <u>must</u> contain an expression of its total error, i.e. both the variance and the bias:

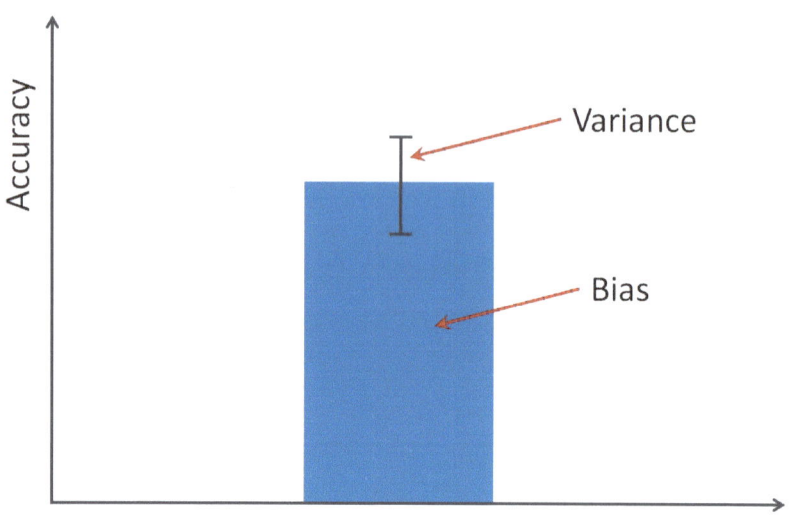

Illustration of the Relationship Between Accuracy, Bias and Variance

This is why any of R^2, variance, MAE and ME cannot on their own fully describe the accuracy of a model – but the RMSE can!

Let's have a look at another couple of models, where this time I've arranged for the RMSE to remain fixed by choosing data from a Pythagorean Triple:

ID	Residuals (Model 4)	Residuals (Model 5)
1	0	3
2	0	3
3	0	3
4	0	3
5	0	3
6	5	4
7	5	4
8	5	4
9	5	4
10	5	4

MAE	MAE
2.5	3.5
Variance	Variance
6.9	0.3
RMSE	RMSE
3.5	3.5

The Bias/Variance Trade-Off in Action!

For a fixed level of accuracy, when you increase the bias (model 5) the variance decreases. This is why it is a trade-off, because **as the variety of the data increases, the bias towards individual data points must decrease**, and *vice versa*.

Do you see what this means?

Since the RMSE has components of bias and variance, it is not enough to smugly quote the RMSE of your model and exclaim 'job done!'. You need to quote the levels of both bias and variance to demonstrate which models (if any) are a good compromise between the competing demands of low bias and low variance.

A model that has low bias and high variance or one with high bias and low variance may have the same overall accuracy but each could produce highly undesirable predictions. It is usually the case (but not always) that **a good compromise between bias and variance leads to the best prediction models**.

Total Accuracy

As far as I'm concerned, you should always **quote the RMSE as the overall measure of the accuracy** of your models. When comparing models to decide which is the most accurate, it's the RMSEs that you compare.

Bias

Next up, you need to **quote the MAE** with an explanation that this tells you by how much each **prediction deviates from observation**.

Then you can **quote the ME** to show whether your model has an **overall bias** – remember that this bias can be positive or negative.

Variance

Finally you can **quote the variance**, explaining that this is a measure of how far your model's **predictions deviate from their average value**.

As an alternative to the variance, you can use R^2. I prefer not to use it because the units are not related to those of your variable of interest, but R^2 is actually a perfectly good choice because most people who are used to running regression analyses will have a good feel for what a good (or bad) R^2 looks like.

If you want to feel smug, you can quote the BVTO – that will usually make you look good in front of the boss...

***

Summary

One Stat to Rule Them All

In this book we've discovered that an **observation** is the measurement of your variable of interest, which is distinct from a **prediction**, which is the outcome of a statistical or Machine Learning algorithm.

A **deviation** is a measure of the difference between an observed value and *some other value*, and we can distinguish between two types of deviations; an **error**, which is derived from the true, unobservable value, while a **residual** is the difference between an observation and a prediction.

The **RMSE** is The Daddy of all the measurements and is, to coin a phrase, **the one stat to rule them all**. I'm sure I've heard that somewhere before...

Anyway, the RMSE is a measure of the **total error of a regression model**, and has components of **bias** and **variance**.

MAE and **ME** are both measures of bias, but differ in that MAE is a measure of the **average size of the residuals**, while ME is an expression of the **average model bias**.

The **R^2 value** and the **variance** are both measures of the variability (variety or variance) of your model. R^2 measures the deviation of predictions **from the line of best fit**, whereas variance is a measure of the **deviation from the residual mean**.

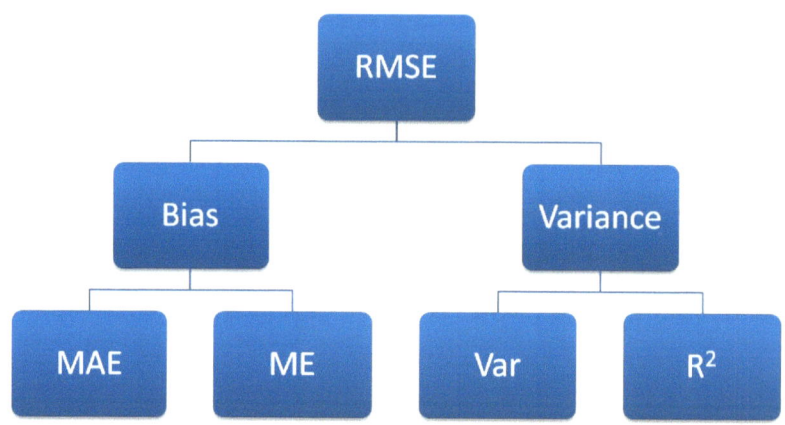

The RMSE Family Tree

I hope that you're now in a much better position to make good choices about measuring the accuracy of your regression models. Better still, the next time you read a comment by Sk8rBoi or RazrButt about the best measures of accuracy you'll break out in a wry grin in the knowledge that not only do you *know* what the correct answer is, but you've got the Bias/Variance Trade-Off as your ally!

***

About The Author

Lee Baker is an award-winning software creator that lives behind a keyboard in a darkened room. Illuminated only by the light from his monitor, he aspires to finding the light switch.

With decades of experience in science, statistics and artificial intelligence, he has a passion for telling stories with data. Despite explaining it a dozen times, his mother still doesn't understand what he does for a living.

Insisting that data analysis is much simpler than we think it is, he authors friendly, easy-to-understand books that teach the fundamentals of data analysis and statistics.

His mission is to unleash your inner data ninja!

As the CEO of Chi-Squared Innovations, one day he'd like to retire to do something simpler, like crocodile wrestling.

http://www.bit.ly/EPMCourse

Leave a Review

Thank you for reading **Errors of Regression Models**.

I hope you enjoyed reading it as much as I enjoyed writing it. If you did, please take a moment to leave a review. The best reviews will be featured at the beginning of the book.

Thank you!

Lee Baker